How to hire a salesperson – successfully

(and what to do if it doesn't work out)

AF133231

How to hire a salesperson – successfully
(and what to do if it doesn't work out)

© Keith Wymer

ISBN: 978-1906316-77-8

All rights reserved.

Published in 2011 by HotHive Books, Evesham, UK.
www.thehothive.com

The right of Keith Wymer to be identified as the author of this work has been asserted by him in accordance with the Copyright, Designs and Patents Act 1988.

A CIP record of this book is available from the British Library.

No part of this publication may be reproduced in any form or by any means without prior permission from the author.

Printed in the UK by Latimer Trend, Plymouth.

Contents

Contents

Page

Introduction ◄ •••••••••••••••••• **07**

1) Planning for a successful hire ◄ •••••• 11
- Planning the nitty gritty: what do you want your salesperson to do?
- Let's start again from the beginning
- Who will generate the sales leads?
- New business or client relationship management?
- What will you measure and what are the rules?
- Salary and commission structure
- Writing a job specification

2) Where to find candidates ◄ ••••••••• 27
- Should I use a recruitment agency?

3) Planning for interviews ◄ ••••••••••• 31
- Before you start, what does a salesperson look and act like?
- Your interview and selection process
- Preparing for interviews
- Managing the first interview
- Preparing for the second interview

Contents

4) From job offer to induction ◄••••••• 43
- Taking references
- Probationary period
- The official paperwork
- Induction

5) When to call it quits and start again ◄•• 49
- When it starts to go wrong

6) Conclusion ◄••••••••••••••••• 53

Introduction

Introduction

I've been running my own businesses for over 20 years and the thing I find most difficult is to find and keep good salespeople.

It has taken me about 15 years to have made enough mistakes to learn from them and work out how to get things right. And when I talk to other business owners, they all say the same thing: "They seem really great at the interview stage and it all starts off well, but then it starts going wrong and you have to let them go."

This book seeks to help you learn from my mistakes so you can minimise the cost and disruption that hiring and firing a salesperson creates.

A word of caution ◀ ● ● ● ● ● ● ● ● ● ● ● ● ● ● ● ● ● ● ●

Just a word of caution though. Always check the legality of anything you want to do concerning the hiring and firing of staff with an expert agency before you take any action. I have an annual contract with such an agency which I sourced through my bank.

Essentially, these agencies will give you advice on personnel issues and, as long as you stick to the letter of their advice, they will insure you against the costs of any industrial tribunals or actions taken against you by employees.

Remember that you're dealing with people, not units of production!

1. Planning for a successful hire

Planning the nitty gritty: what do you want your salesperson to do?

A common reason for salespeople failing is that the boss hasn't worked out what is expected of them and/or has failed to communicate this clearly.

Like so many obvious things, this part is really hard to do and you should keep challenging yourself and asking yourself to explain and justify what you mean. For example, when asked what they want their salesperson to do, many people say "Pick up the phone and talk to prospects. Then I want them to get out there and bring home the orders."

Now, that's a good start but it's just a framework, not a plan, and a framework will only lead to miscommunication between you and your salesperson.

This is particularly true if you hire an experienced salesperson, who will tend to do what they have done elsewhere – which may not be right for your business. And who says they were doing the right things in their old job?

Challenge yourself!

When you say you want them to pick up the phone, who do you want them to call? How many conversations should they have in a day? Are they supposed to be selling on the phone or making appointments to go out and see people? Are they really just to talk or do you want some measurable activity from the call, such as mentioning this month's promotion?

I've found in recent years that picking up the phone on its own is no longer cost effective unless you're dealing with existing customers. The dynamics of marketing have changed and your new salesperson is more likely to enjoy sales success by following up inbound leads generated by your website or other marketing and advertising activities.

Clarify your intentions
When you say you want them to go out there and bring home the orders, which products or services should the orders be for? How many orders and for how much value? How soon after they join you do you expect them to get an order? What will you do if they unearth an opportunity outside your normal range of offerings?

Let's start again from the beginning ◀ • • • • • •
So let's start again with working out what you want your salesperson to do.

To make our example easy to understand, let's say you sell something tangible, such as cleaning materials (this part of your planning is a bit harder if you offer bespoke services). We want our salesperson to follow up sales leads which should result in an appointment where they can demonstrate the excellence of our cleaning materials.

The first question to answer is who we want the salesperson to sell to. This means we must specify the typical decision-maker job title in each of the vertical markets we service. For example, "I want my salesperson to sell to facilities managers and general managers in laboratories, factories and offices of at least 6000sq ft in a 50-mile radius from our office."

Excellent! We have defined the salesperson's target market. When you appoint someone, you no longer have to worry about them going down blind alleys in their search for sales or coming up with the old line about "I know I can get an order from my old contact Jim Jones," who needs a difficult product mix and whose geographical location creates all kinds of logistical and margin-reducing activities for you.

Over the years I have allowed numerous salespeople to lead me to their old customers and it has always ended in customer dissatisfaction. When you think about it, if they were the right customers for you, they would already be dealing with you or at least be aware of you.

So be very careful about deviating from your target market, even though your new hire sells the idea convincingly to you.

Remember – they are a salesperson. They're just doing their job! Make sure you do yours as a manager.

It's OK to disappoint your salesperson. It will only demotivate them for a short while and it is important for you to show confidence in your decision-making ability. So from day one you can say "I want you to sell to facilities managers and general managers in laboratories, factories and offices of at least 6000sq ft in a 50-mile radius from our office and **no-one else**."

If it turns out you've got the target market wrong, it's up to you to change it, not your salesperson. Experience has taught me that unless you give absolutely explicit instructions to your salesperson about who they should be selling to, they'll use a scattergun approach which will fail.

Who will generate the sales leads?

Now we're able to concentrate on the generation of sales leads. This is fundamentally important before you start thinking about hiring someone in order to maximise the chances of your new salesperson succeeding.

First we need to ask, "What is a lead?" In some businesses it will be where the prospect agrees to see the salesperson even though they have nothing going on at the moment. In another, a lead will be where the prospect has a stated buying need with a budget and timescale.

You need to decide what you consider a lead to be. This is for you to decide, not your salesperson. In business-to-business selling, I have always believed a lead is where the prospect has a proven need for what we sell, a budget, a timescale and a clearly defined decision-making unit. In business-to-consumer selling, I prefer to define a lead as where the enquirer has specified what they're looking for and has a phone number and email address. Your own definition may be different, but the important thing is to communicate it clearly to your new salesperson.

Once you have defined what you believe a lead to be, you need to work out whether you want your salesperson to generate leads or whether to give that task to someone else. Although it's not always possible, ideally your salesperson should just follow up leads, not generate them. Lead generation is really a marketing function and marketing is a separate skill from selling. Your salesperson may not have marketing skills (although most of them think they have!).

Also, think carefully about how much lead generation is the salesperson's responsibility because these activities will eat into their selling time. It is often dangerous to let your new hire find their own leads because it is very time consuming and you are likely to lose faith in them before they start delivering a return on your investment. By that I mean you may see them prospecting but you won't see much selling, so you could start to lose heart. This usually starts a downward spiral which results in the salesperson being deemed a failure by the end of their trial period.

If you must involve your salesperson in lead generation, using the phone to follow up web leads is the obvious choice and we'll return to this in a moment, but what about direct mail, e-shots, trade fairs, off-the page advertising, door knocking, leafleting, networking and the web? Do you expect your salesperson to use any or all of these media and if so, how much time should they allocate to each? If you don't specify, the salesperson will concentrate on those they find most enjoyable or where they have previously enjoyed success. The problem here is that if you let the salesperson allocate your resources, you may run out of budget!

Returning to following up web leads by phone (which is often the task salespeople like the least, although they won't tell you this!), do you have a large enough quantity of usable leads with phone numbers for the salesperson to be productive? If they use up the leads too quickly because there are too few of them, they'll have nothing to do and will become demotivated. It's your responsibility to feed them with more than enough leads to keep them rolling. If you don't know how many leads they'll need, either try prospecting yourself for a few hours (at least three hours when you do nothing else) or ask an experienced sales manager in another organisation for their best estimate.

New business or client relationship management?

Then we have to establish the answer to another key question: are salespeople required to develop relationships with their new clients or are they supposed to be prospecting only for new business and handing their new clients over to someone else for relationship management? The question of relationship management is interesting. Once you have won a customer, of course you want to develop a relationship. But decide before hiring a new salesperson whether or not managing the ongoing relationship will be their responsibility or that of someone else.

> **My advice, if you can, would be to split new business sales and relationship management into two separate jobs done by two different people.**

If you hire a new business salesperson and allow them to become an order taker, you're not maximising your investment in that person. So now we come to the question of how you will measure the effectiveness of your new hire, because you will need to set both your expectations and theirs before you take someone on.

What will you measure and what are the rules?

Another obvious but frequently overlooked question is: Assuming that the salesperson will make phone calls to follow up web leads, what is the goal of the call? Should they try to sell the products on the phone or do you want them to go out and demonstrate them or even take specifications for a more complicated offering? You must be explicit about whether they are telesales or field sales people, or a mixture of both.

How many sales or appointments should they expect to make per day, month or quarter? Before interviewing anyone, make sure you have created achievable, measurable targets for their activities so that everyone knows what's expected right from the start.

It is OK to share these targets during interviews because if they are unrealistic, the candidates should ask you to explain what support they would get to help reach them. That's a big clue for you that your targets may be unrealistic.

> **A handy tip for when you are interviewing is if the general consensus is that the targets are high but one candidate doesn't feel they are, don't hire them because they will disappoint you when in the job.**

They obviously need the job so badly they're prepared to take a short-term view and they'll end up getting fired early on for underperformance. Having listened to your interviewees, if your targets remain unrealistic, it will quickly become apparent after the person starts working for you and you can always adjust them, but you need to have specified the parameters for success before hiring anyone.

It is also important to think about the style in which you want your salesperson to communicate. When they're on the phone, what do you want them to say? Although most salespeople will jib at being given a script to use, it's very important that you tell them the message you want to communicate as well as the style of the communication.

On a more general note, if you don't like the way a candidate sounds or dresses, don't hire them. Your target market will have evolved a style that is appropriate for it and you will be part of that evolution. If a candidate is wrong for you, they will be wrong for your market too.

Let us now assume that your sales process will require a face-to-face meeting:

- What will you expect from your new salesperson? How do you expect them to dress for the appointment? Should men wear a tie?
- What sales aids will you make available such as a laptop presentation (again this is one for you to create), samples, business cards, etc? Here I'm talking about all the tangible tools the salesperson will need to be successful.
- What are the rules that need to be obeyed when the salesperson is out on the road? For example, how often should they check in with the office?
- What is your minimum order and mix of products? How will they know what is in stock when they are out on the road? How much authority will they have to offer discounts?

Once you have identified the answers to these questions, you can build them into interview questions to establish what the candidate feels is right in this kind of job. If their answers don't match your expectations, don't hire them.

Next we need to determine exactly what the salesperson will be required to sell. Returning to our cleaning materials example, is the range of products restricted? By that I mean are special orders for bespoke materials to be handled by you or the salesperson? Will they have a minimum order value?

By now, you should have enough material to communicate effectively what the salesperson will do when they join you. This is a big step in ensuring that you hire the correct person and that they will be sufficiently successful to want to stay with you.

Salary and commission structure ◄ • • • • • • • • • •

If you're to attract and keep a good salesperson, you'll need to devise an attractive salary and commission package. If you're unsure of how much to pay, something to be wary of when you are writing a job spec is that one is often tempted to ask the recruitment agency for advice on salary levels.

A recruitment consultant will always give you the top end of the pay range because they will be on commission and will make more money on a higher starting salary. It is also easier for the recruiter to attract candidates if they're offering jobs with over-inflated salaries.

It's better to do your own research on the web where salary levels are concerned. The same is true over the job title. Agencies often suggest you call the role "Sales Manager" or "Sales Executive" because it makes it easier to sell to candidates. Beware. If it's not a sales manager's role, don't say it is because it sets candidates' expectations incorrectly and you'll attract the wrong people for the job.

When I set salary levels, experience has taught me that a good rule of thumb is to offer approximately 5% less than the highest salaries around for the job but to pay the best commission rates. This is because I want to attract hungry people who will help me drive the business forward. Paying a higher than average commission helps me identify who is more of a risk-taker and therefore in line with the goals of my business.

If you're new to hiring salespeople, you may be asking why you should have to pay commission at all. After all, if I pay them well, why don't they just do their job like anyone else? The reason is that a certain type of person is attracted to the idea of commission and in my experience they usually make good salespeople.

I always create tiered commission systems where the better the salesperson's performance, the higher the commission level they receive. For example, in one of my businesses, I pay 2.5% commission on everything up to target, but that increases to 3% on everything the moment target is exceeded. I also offer accelerator bonuses for performance over target to get the salespeople to really stretch themselves. For example, in my retail business, they get a set bonus up to 9.9% over target, double that for being 10% over target, and so on up to 30% over target.

In order to minimise disputes over "stealing" leads and other competitive shenanigans, I also offer a further bonus if everybody hits target, to encourage the salespeople to help each other.

Having worked out the remuneration package, we have to write a job specification to give to agencies.

Writing a job specification ◀ • • • • • • • • • • • • • •

The job specification follows on from the document where you have specified what you want the salesperson to do, and its function is to enable you to briefly communicate to potential employees and to agencies the details of what you are looking for. In the job specification, you should specify the job title, location, salary, on target earnings (OTE), whether there is a car and any other benefits. Don't forget to include the typical working hours and holiday entitlement.

Most importantly, give a brief description of what the salesperson will be required to do. You can always attach your longer planning document as well if you wish, but generally one to two pages is plenty for the job description.

Example of a job specification

Holborn Training – Corporate Sales Executive	
The company:	We are a small, family-owned business operating as an office skills training centre in WC1.
	We provide self-paced training courses plus seminars in all subjects related to secretarial, administrative, bookkeeping and IT staff.
	Ours is the oldest and best-known brand in office skills training.
The role:	The role for which we are recruiting is critical to maintaining our breathtaking sales success.
	We need a talented individual with great communication skills, to follow up and convert enquiries from large organisations in London with the aim of selling training courses. We see this as a totally new business sales role, with no ongoing customer relationship management.
	It is likely that larger opportunities will require an element of face-to-face selling.

1. Planning for a successful hire

The person:	We seek an open-minded individual who is willing to learn from us how to approach the corporate market. A hardworking person with a positive attitude will quickly learn to be successful and will be welcomed as a member of our 15-person company.
The hours:	09:00–17:30 Monday to Friday.
Support:	The new team member will receive one day's formal sales training followed by a considerable number of hours of on-the-job coaching during the first month.
Targets:	The successful new joiner will be targeted on the number of appointments generated per week and the value of sales won.
Salary:	£25,000 pa plus commission. OTE £40K.

2. Where to find candidates

2. Where to find candidates

Should I use a recruitment agency? ◄ • • • • • • •

I spent years pondering over whether I was right to use a recruitment agency. Experience has now taught me that you should, even though it will cost you a lot of money! The reason I recommend agencies is that quality candidates will usually come via this route. I believe this is because good people will know that serious employers will go to an agency – it's where the jobs are!

When you are looking at agencies, you will learn that many will offer a rebate should the new hire not work out. The rebate will usually be for a period of 12 weeks from the date the candidate starts and will decrease by the week. For example, you might get 100% of the recruitment fee if the candidate leaves in the first week, decreasing to 5% if they leave in the 12th week.

Many agencies offer a free replacement service where, should the candidate not work out in the first 12 weeks of employment, they will find you a replacement free of charge instead of a rebate. In my experience, it is better to have the free replacement than the rebate. This is because you will know in the first 12 weeks whether the salesperson is going to be right for you and you don't want to pay a second recruitment fee if your first choice leaves or gets fired.

Some people, when they appoint an agency, like the comfort of knowing they can reclaim at least part of the recruitment fee should the candidate leave but this is looking at the opportunity from the wrong angle. There is no point waiting for, say, eight weeks before deciding that your new hire is wrong for you and then receiving 25% of the recruitment fee, because you'll then have to recruit a replacement at the full agency fee.

On the subject of recruitment fees, I have paid anything from 15% to 30% of the annual starting salary and the more specialised the sales role you need to fill, the more you should expect to pay.

Apart from using recruitment agencies, I have also tried advertising in newspapers but, to be truthful, I have found that this has always attracted the jobseekers the agencies have rejected. The cost of advertising tends to be nearly as much as an agency fee if you want an advert that reflects well on your organisation, but you have to pay for it whether you are successful in filling your vacancy or not.

From time to time, other employees or friends and family will point a candidate in your direction. These candidates must be handled in exactly the same way as total strangers, but experience has taught me that it's best to not even interview them. This is because if it doesn't work out and you have to fire them, the person recommending them will be offended and the pain is worse than a very high recruitment agency fee.

Few salespeople can resist the flattery of being headhunted.

You'll need someone else to make the headhunting phone call and the initial screening meeting, but essentially all you have to do is have your colleague call someone you have your eye on and say that they have been headhunted and would they like to talk about a potentially exciting role at a rival organisation. If you don't have your eye on someone specific, just call your rival's sales department and make the same pitch with the salesperson who handles your call. You can also ask them whether there is anyone else in the department you should approach. You can ask some qualifying questions to ensure that you're not talking to the boss!

3. Planning for interviews

Before you start, what does a salesperson look and act like?

The first point to understand is that a successful salesperson does not necessarily have "the gift of the gab". Successful salespeople exhibit all kinds of personality traits but garrulousness is rarely one of them.

It's always great if they have charm and grace, but these gifts are less important than the ability to listen and respond with answers outlining what is in it for the customer or prospect to buy from them. Some of the most successful salespeople I have hired have been quiet types, low responders, or people a little lacking in social skills but with an amazing ability to listen actively and/or intuitively to what the prospect is trying to communicate to them.

So look for someone who listens, thinks, responds and is persuasive in an assertive rather than an aggressive way. These traits are rather difficult to spot because they're subtle, but if you interview six salespeople you're likely to find someone who displays some of these characteristics. That doesn't mean you should hire that person.

You should just be aware that you are learning what a good salesperson looks and acts like as you continue your search for the right person.

Your interview and selection process

There are so many variables in hiring a salesperson that a little forward planning for interviews will help you be successful.

Step one is to think about when you would like the new person to start. This is usually more difficult than you would imagine, because it will use up a lot of your own time that you would normally spend on your own part of the business. So you need to think about three things:

1. How much time it will take to complete the interview process.
2. How much notice the successful candidate will need to give to their current employer before joining you.
3. When and how long it will take you to induct the new sales person.

The interview process will take you a minimum of six weeks and probably longer.

I base this on the agency sending you a number of CVs to read. You will need to decide how many of these candidates you want to interview. If you don't know, see them all so you can refine what you're looking for. Once you've told the agency who you want to see, it will take several days for them to arrange interviews for you (we'll talk about interviewing shortly). You'll need to hold second interviews which will take you into a third week.

When you find someone you'd like to hire, it will take a while for you to take references. Most candidates will have to give a month's notice to their current employer while some require three months, and then you can more or less write off your own time in the first month they join.

So you need to plan sufficiently far ahead, allowing for notice periods and the possibility that it may take you longer than you wanted to find the right person. In most cases, you can expect your interview and selection process to take 6 to 12 weeks.

Preparing for interviews

For most people, life and work get in the way of preparing for interviews and it is almost a surprise when the first interviewee arrives. This is a shame because you end up learning your interview technique on-the-job and that means you are wasting the opportunity to get the best out of each candidate. A poor interviewer can turn a perfect candidate into an also-ran, leaving you with a smaller pool of talent from which to choose and may result in a very expensive wrong choice. When the agency sends you a batch of CVs, read each one carefully. Many CVs will list milestones such as "Successfully increased sales by 120% in two years". This is great, but you need to find out two things:

- How was this achieved? What were the processes and actions that were implemented to achieve this result?
- What kinds of numbers are we talking about? After all, 120% growth on £100 isn't very impressive!

Go through the CV with a fine tooth comb and every time something stands out, write on it a question, asking for a detailed description of the how, what and why of every statement made. Don't forget to write on the CV the question of why they want to leave their current job. Just as you had to challenge yourself when creating your job specification and supporting information, you need to challenge your candidates.

Managing the first interview ◀ • • • • • • • • • • • • •
This is your opportunity to decide whether to invest a great deal of money, time and energy in the most important person in your business. Spend that opportunity wisely. It's a given that the candidate will be nervous, but it's OK for you to be nervous too.

You're about to take a gamble and the purpose of this book is to tilt the odds in your favour.

When you meet the candidate for the first time, go through all the normal social courtesies and then take control of the interview by talking for four to six minutes about your organisation and the job. This should be plenty of time because the candidate will have received the job specification from the agency and you should expect them to have also researched your website.

After your brief introduction, ease the prospect gently into the questions you have written on their CV. Your goal now is to get the candidate talking so that you can listen and learn about the nuts and bolts of what they have achieved elsewhere. While the candidate is talking, have a quick look to see whether you approve of the way they are turned out – your customers will!

You should also have prepared questions related to their styles and behaviours as mentioned earlier in this book. I also like to ask questions such as "What will your next major purchase be?" and "What will your retirement look like?", because I want to see how money hungry they are.

I'm always suspicious of salespeople who say they're not motivated by money, because it suggests their comfort level is too easily achieved so they won't stretch themselves for you. I like to hire people who have large mortgages, school fees or even some kind of a secret they don't want to share but which indicates they need to earn as much commission as possible.

At the time of writing, I have two salespeople on my team who are new arrivals to our country and they both have a burning desire to earn lots of money and make something of themselves. Their naked ambition is very appealing and is paying off as they work long and hard.

Another useful line of questioning is to quiz the candidates on their innate understanding of sales technique. I always ask them what are the steps of the sales process in their current role, to see whether they have a structured approach to selling as I personally believe this is important in building success.

Having established the steps of the sale, I ask them to flesh out some basic points of sales technique, such as "What is the difference between open and closed questions?", "What is the difference between a feature and a benefit?" and "What do you say when a prospect says they 'want to think about it'?"

If they get the answers wrong, it's not necessarily a deal breaker, but it will make me ponder how the salesperson can be successful in their current role if they haven't fully grasped the basics, and it also gives me an idea as to how much training I will have to deliver in addition to product training.

It's a question of identifying how fully formed the candidate is at the time of the interview.

If they don't have any prepared questions, don't hire them. They haven't been sufficiently interested in your opportunity to do any research. Similarly, even if they appear to be great salespeople, if they succeed in dominating you during the interview, don't hire them because you won't be able to manage them if they join you and they'll make your life a misery. If they are also looking at non-sales jobs, I wouldn't hire them because they are looking for an easier job than the one you are offering.

If they are close to receiving an offer from another organisation, you'll know how quickly you'll have to move if you want them. By the way, it's not worth asking "How does our role stack up? If I was able to offer you the job today, would you take it?" The candidate has little choice but to say yes, but they can go back to the agency and say no.

Whether or not you intend to invite the candidate back for a second interview, it's worth explaining that there will be a second interview during which a presentation will be required. If you want them to come back, tell them what the presentation will be about. If you're not sure whether you want to see them again, explain that the agency will tell them what it will be about.

Two final points about first interviews relate directly to you and your behaviour:

- First, be aware that you are also more likely to remember the first and last candidates you see – it's human nature! I bet most salespeople who get hired have been either first or last to be seen.

- Second, you are likely to get bored asking the same questions repeatedly and will pay less attention to candidates in the middle of your interview list.

Both of these factors are a bit unfair on the other candidates and you run the risk of hiring the wrong person. Force yourself to concentrate harder on the candidates who are in the middle of your list and make lots of notes about each to help you remember them. Make your decision to decline any candidates quickly so they don't cloud your memory and decision-making process, leaving you fresh enough to concentrate on the ones with potential.

Preparing for the second interview ◀ • • • • • • •

When it comes to the second interview presentation, give them a topic related to your business for which they will need to research further.

There is very little value in getting them to demonstrate how to sell a pen or some similar item. You want to see whether they are keen enough to bother preparing something specifically for your vacancy. Tell them they can deliver the presentation in any format they wish – ie PowerPoint, flipchart, etc – but be clear that part of your decision-making process will rest on this.

The second interview is often more difficult to prepare for than the first, because you already have so much information on the candidate. Even so, it is worth structuring the interview in order to give you the chance to compare the remaining candidates.

I usually open by asking what questions the candidate has wondered about since the first interview. If they don't have any at this stage, it's not the end of the world but it is a good opportunity for them to get their questions out in the open. If they don't have any questions, they may not be sufficiently hungry for your role.

Next, realising they are going to be nervous about it, I invite them to give their presentation. I am always unimpressed if they don't bring any prepared items with them, but it is always possible that they have the rare ability to be able to wing it.

3. Planning for interviews

During the presentation I am looking to see how closely they understood the brief, at the quality of their research and for any clues to suggest how hungry they are for the job. I also want to see how they sell themselves under pressure. I'm not put off by nervousness, but I want to see some hint of a structured approach to their presentation.

If I'm impressed, I'm often prepared to invest a small sum in a psychometric test (downloaded from the web) immediately. Some of these are free while others require a small fee. While these tests do not always help, they remove more variables from my decision-making process. These tests work by quickly and easily enabling you to create a profile of the characteristics and behaviours that best fit the job specification and to profile the candidate against those yardsticks.

Next, return to the candidate's CV and open the questioning by asking what their former employers would have to say about them. I then ask a number of questions that I believe are pertinent to the job:

- "Talk me through the full process you use in a typical sales meeting."
- "Have you ever had a situation where a prospect wouldn't let you stick to your usual routine? What happened? What did you do?"
- "What's the biggest deal you've ever done? What did it feel like?"

- "How much value have you sold this year?"
- "Last time we met, you said money wasn't your main motivation. What is? How do you measure it?"
- "What emotions do you think your current boss would experience if you handed in your notice?"
- "How many of your past clients would welcome a call from you if you were in a new job? How many would want to see you for a presentation?"
- "What is the most frustrating thing that has ever happened to you related to a sale and why? What did you do about it?"
- "Have you ever rescued a lost sale? How did you do it?"
- "Have you ever worked in a start-up situation before? If yes, what were the best and worst things about it?"

Next, I ask them to explain what training they think they will require to be effective in the job. This means the training and support they feel will be important for them to be successful. If they struggle to answer this (it's quite difficult for them to identify what they don't know), ask them to describe the training support they got in the sales job in which they were most successful.

4. From job offer to induction

Taking references ◀ ● ● ● ● ● ● ● ● ● ● ● ● ● ● ● ●

Once you have identified who you want to hire, you can make them an offer conditional on references.

These days, official references don't always have great value because the referee is not allowed to divulge much, but they can help to show attendance patterns. You're probably better off speaking directly with the candidate's previous line managers. In particular, it's what they don't say that's important. If the references don't stack up, withdraw your job offer. At the same time, don't forget to check Google and Facebook to see whether there are any entries on there that would make you change your mind about the person.

Probationary period ◀ ● ● ● ● ● ● ● ● ● ● ● ● ● ● ● ●

It is important to have a probationary period for your new hire and I normally recommend three months.

Within three months you'll know whether or not you have hired the right person for the job, even if your sales cycle is longer than that.

Some people say that if you're in doubt at this stage, you can always offer an extension to the probationary period but, in my experience, you're better off terminating the salesperson than prolonging the agony. If you have negotiated a free replacement deal with your employment agency, it will usually expire within three months so this is your opportunity to make the most of that.

During the probationary period I always stipulate that only one week's notice is required from either side and this rises to a month after the probationary period.

The probationary period is interesting because the job frequently evolves during this time. For example, the salesperson's list of suspects should have developed into a prospect list and by now there should be some intent to buy on the part of the prospects.

So the role has moved from prospecting to selling and it is important to see how the salesperson adapts to this in order for you to decide whether to keep them.

The official paperwork ◀ ● ● ● ● ● ● ● ● ● ● ● ● ● ● ●

Once again, it's best to get your personnel service to write the contract of employment, but remember that the employee is entitled to such a contract by law.

In addition to an offer letter and a contract of employment, you are likely to have a company employment manual which provides detailed information on the company's disciplinary procedures, car policy and so on.

One of the most frequently overlooked documents is the one listing the assets you are going to lend to the salesperson to enable them to do their job.

In this document you will list the company car – including make, model and registration number, details of laptops or tablet computers and any other expensive items you provide. This is because, if it should all go wrong, you will have a better chance of recovering these items than if they are not signed for.

Induction

Your own work is just about to begin! Your expensive new hire will need a lot of early support to enable them to be successful, even if they're an experienced salesperson. The first week or so will require you to role-model the behaviours and processes the salesperson will be required to implement, so you'll have to be on your best behaviour!

The salesperson will be eager to please and will want to add value, frequently saying: "Wouldn't it be better if we did it this way? It worked at my last place." Your response should be: "Well, let's start off this way to give us a base to work from, then we can adjust it later as we get to know more." This will be your first attempt to manage the salesperson and it will pay dividends as it is a gentle way of saying you know best but you're adaptable.

Product training is an important part of the induction but, because this is detail rich, it tends to be a bit boring. For this reason, just concentrate on your top 10 selling items. A lot of this early training will be forgotten and by concentrating on just a few items the sales person will absorb more data.

They can pick up the rest of the information when they know what they're talking about.

Never let your new salesperson, no matter how experienced, handle a phone call or go out on an appointment without you being there for the first few weeks. You'll need to role-model the phone style and the appointment style for the salesperson to make sure they're doing it your way. They can always adapt and improve it later but their lack of knowledge of your specific situation means you need a base line to start from.

Over the first few weeks you need to move from you role-modelling to being a double act and finally the salesperson role-modelling for you. Once you're happy with the way they're performing, you can let them loose on their own.

After three months, be sure to put them on a short, formal sales training course. This is because they will have developed a mixture of your style and their own by this point and their messages to customers and prospects will be confusing. A short course will straighten them out. Most salespeople at this stage begin to make shortcuts in the questioning stage of the sale, as well as confusing features with benefits. Make sure the course on which you send them covers these subjects in detail.

5. When to call it quits and start again

5. When to call it quits and start again

When it starts to go wrong

I'm sorry to report that even after taking more than reasonable care, I have lived through this phase many times.

What usually happens is that the relationship starts warmly. After all, both employer and employee want everything to work out well. There is the honeymoon period where the employer is really pleased with their new hire and I have often seen the new salesperson enjoy some "beginner's luck" and win an early success.

It is usually after the first month (sometimes earlier) that the shine starts to rub off. You'll get the feeling that the salesperson either hasn't got their heart in it or they're reinventing the wheel or there will be some other issue that makes you feel uneasy. Often it's not anything quantifiable, just a feeling that the salesperson may not work out in the longer term.

It is vital to communicate with your employee to avoid a gulf opening up between the pair of you. If your discussion identifies a gap in the salesperson's knowledge base or skill set, you can deal with it and put everything back on an even keel.

If the problem is attitudinal or psychological, at least a discussion will alert the salesperson to the fact that you are displeased and it gives them a chance to demonstrate different behaviours. The point is that you'll both feel better for having addressed the issue and it gives you the chance to move forward.

5. When to call it quits and start again

Now, before I give you my next piece of advice, I should stress that I run past every disciplinary problem with our employment law advisors, just to make sure that I'm keeping everything legal.

By the beginning of month three, the salesperson should be showing real value in a measurable sense and should have integrated into the business on a personal level. If they haven't, you're better off cutting your losses and hiring somebody else.

You'll have to think of your lost recruitment agency fee as an "education fee" because you should have learned something about hiring a salesperson. If you've negotiated a free replacement deal with your agency, this is the time to use it.

I know that sounds glib, but I remember clearly my own mentality during these times. Most of us try to justify the continued employment of the salesperson to ourselves:

- "Well, it's still early days."
- "I'll give them another month and then decide."
- "They've just bought a new flat so it would be cruel to do it now."
- "Maybe I should do the training all over again."
- "The market must be flat at the moment."
- "I don't think I'm psychologically strong enough to fire them."

5. When to call it quits and start again

It's quite normal to go through all these things in your head, but I have found that in every case when I have lost confidence in a salesperson, I'm still thinking the same thoughts in months four, five and six. And by that time you've wasted a ton of sales leads and pushed back the window of opportunity for recruiting a replacement.

With due respect to HR experts and to employment law, experience has taught me that it is better to lose a new salesperson early and start again rather than hoping you'll be able to turn things round.

6. Conclusion

6. Conclusion

Hiring a salesperson is really difficult – and expensive! The purpose of this book has been to outline how much effort needs to go into minimising the risk of failure.

The bottom line is that you are dealing with a particular type of human being and all the unpredictability that brings.

The best you can do is apply the structures and disciplines I have suggested to help you make the best choices you can.

To summarise:

- Plan ahead and identify in detail what you want your salesperson to do.
- Work out your salary and commission structure and make it attractive to hungry people.
- Write a job specification so that all interested parties are singing from the same hymn sheet.
- Use a recruitment agency for best value even though the cost seems high.
- Expect a realistic (ie lengthy) timescale for the recruitment process and craft your interview questions and actions in advance.

6. Conclusion

- Be aware that you are more likely to remember the first and last candidates you see, and compensate for this with those in the middle of your list.
- Never hire anyone who doesn't ask you any questions.
- Get the offer paperwork right in case you need to terminate the new salesperson early.
- If it all goes wrong, it's cheaper and more efficient to let them go early and start again than to keep putting off a painful decision.

Best of luck!